I Love

Tractors & Diggers

By Lisa Regan
Illustrated by Alan Hancocks

First published in 2008 by Miles Kelly Publishing Ltd
Bardfield Centre, Great Bardfield, Essex, CM7 4SL

Copyright © Miles Kelly Publishing Ltd 2008

2 4 6 8 10 9 7 5 3 1

Editorial Director Belinda Gallagher
Art Director Jo Brewer
Editorial Assistant Toby Tippen
Designers Michelle Canatella, Carmen Johnson
Cover Artworker Carmen Johnson
Production Manager Elizabeth Brunwin
Reprographics Stephan Davis, Ian Paulyn

ISBN 978-1-84810-039-8

Printed in Thailand

ACKNOWLEDGEMENTS
Page 7 Joe Gough/Fotolia.com; 20 Antonella
Grandoni/Fotolia.com; 23 SemA/Fotolia.com
All other images from the Miles Kelly Archives

British Library Cataloguing-in-Publication Data
A catalogue record for this book is available
from the British Library

Made with paper from a sustainable forest

www.mileskelly.net   info@mileskelly.net

www.factsforprojects.com

Contents

Baler

In summer, the farmer uses a machine called a baler to help him collect straw. Pulled by a tractor, the baler squashes the cut straw into bales, which are large bundles of tied-up straw. The bales are stored in a barn or piled up in a field.

Wrapped up

Bales may be wrapped in black plastic. The plastic keeps the straw dry.

The baler rolls and ties up the straw, and drops the finished bale out of the back.

As well as a baler, a tractor can pull different machines, such as grass mowers, ploughs, and crop sprayers.

As the tractor drives across the field, the baler picks up the straw.

5

Potato harvester

It takes a lot of work to get a potato from the ground and onto your plate! A tractor pulls a huge harvesting machine that digs up the potatoes and shakes off the dirt. The potatoes are dropped into a trailer and taken away to be packaged for the shops.

Most of the soil falls off the potatoes as they are carried along a large belt towards the end of the trailer.

Large metal discs underneath the harvester dig into the ground and throw up the potatoes.

Harvesting huge fields can take a long time. Farmers sometimes carry on collecting their crops into the night.

The potatoes travel up a kind of escalator on the harvester. They are collected in a truck that is driven slowly alongside.

Potato meals
How many different ways can you think of cooking potatoes?

Scraper

In building work, a scraper is a big machine that is used to help flatten the ground. It scrapes up soil so that building work, such as making dams, bridges and roads, can begin. A scraper can move lots of soil at once.

The bowl part of a scraper that holds the soil is called a hopper.

A large metal blade scrapes across the dirt to dig it up and makes the ground smooth and level.

The driver sits in a cab at the front. It has windows and doors to stop dirt and dust getting inside.

Shape up

The slopes and flat fairways on golf courses are often shaped by a scraper.

9

Forklift tractor

When a forklift is attached to a tractor, it can lift heavy loads, such as bales of hay. A forklift has two metal forks that slide beneath a load. The driver can then operate the forklift to move the load up or down.

The forks slide underneath loads that are too big, heavy or high for a person to lift.

Stacking up

A different kind of forklift vehicle can be used to stack large objects in factories and warehouses.

These metal rods are called pistons. They slide in and out like a telescope to move the forklift up and down.

Bulldozer

This strong, heavy machine is used to clear and level ground. It is often seen helping to build new roads. A bulldozer has a big scoop to push heavy loads out of the way. It can move rocks and soil, too.

The driver uses push-and-pull levers to operate the bulldozer.

Instead of wheels, a bulldozer has caterpillar tracks. These make it easier for the bulldozer to drive over slippery ground such as mud or snow.

Vehicles with caterpillar tracks are sometimes called 'crawlers' because of the way they move slowly along.

On track

Army tanks have caterpillar tracks to help them travel over bumpy ground during battle.

The most powerful bulldozers can push more than 216 tonnes – that's the same as pushing about 70 elephants!

This bulldozer is using its scoop to collect a large pile of salt in a salt mine.

13

Plough

A farmer ploughs his fields before he plants new seeds in the soil. The plough is a large farming tool with blades that cut through the earth and turn it over. Any grass, weeds or old plants are buried and the soil is ready to grow new crops.

Ploughing is best done in dry weather. If the field is wet, it is too difficult to dig and turn the soil.

The blades must be sharp to cut through the grass and soil.

The tractor is driven up and down the field, pulling the plough in a straight line. It makes grooves in the soil called furrows.

Hydraulic hammer

This machine is also known as a rock breaker. A big hammer is attached to the front of a digger to smash up rocks and buildings. The workers on the building site have to wear ear protectors because the noise is so loud.

Bird hammer

Woodpeckers break into trees by hammering them with their beaks. They then feed on the insects found inside.

The strongest hammers can smash concrete floors or walls by hitting them 45 times in a minute.

171

Backhoe loader

This kind of digger can do lots of jobs. It has a large bucket at the front for moving earth and rocks, and a small one at the back for digging holes and trenches. Trenches are long, thin ditches for pipes to go in.

This small bucket is the backhoe. It can be changed for other tools, such as a grapple, which is a metal claw that picks things up.

A loader often scoops rocks and earth into the back of a dump truck. The truck takes the dirt away and tips it out.

Auger

An auger can drill deep holes and remove the dirt at the same time. It is used to make holes for fence posts or tall poles for buildings. The spiral-shaped drill can be fixed to the front of a digger or a tractor.

Small holes

Builders can fix shelves to walls inside houses by drilling holes with a hand-held drill. It works in very a similar way to the auger.

The strong metal screw spins very quickly. It drills down through the ground and lifts out soil as it twists.

Augers dig deep, round holes. A digger can't make such neat circular holes.

The driver sits in a cab and operates the auger controls to move the arm up and down.

Bucket-wheel excavator

These massive machines are the largest moving vehicles in the world. It can take five years to build just one! They are used in mines to dig coal out of the ground. The coal is loaded onto a long conveyor belt to move it to where it is needed.

Each part of the excavator has caterpillar tracks so it can be moved around.

A bucket-wheel excavator is so huge that it can take weeks to move the machine to a new place.

Moving on

Conveyor belts have many uses, such as moving drinks bottles in factories.

A conveyor belt is a bit like an escalator that travels in a straight line. It moves all the time, taking the coal along with it.

The giant wheel has lots of buckets on it. Each bucket scoops up coal or soil and drops it onto a conveyor belt.

Fun facts

Baling Hay and straw bales are different. Hay is grass that has been cut and dried. Straw is the leftover stalks after corn has been harvested.

Harvesting Not all crops are harvested in the same way as potatoes. Cereals such as wheat and barley are cut with the sharp blades of a combine harvester.

Scraper If a scraper gets stuck, a bulldozer can be used to push it free.

Forklift tractor A forklift often carries heavy items on a wooden rack called a pallet, which slides on and off the forks.

Bulldozer Large building site vehicles cost a lot of money. A bulldozer costs more than a Ferrari sports car – that's over £100,000!

Ploughing After the farmer has ploughed his field, he may pull a harrow behind the tractor to break large lumps of soil into smaller pieces. Harrowing makes the soil more suitable for planting seeds in.

Hydraulic hammer Sometimes, these hammers are used in mining. They break up rocks containing precious metals, jewels or fuel, such as coal.

Backhoe loader The driver's seat can spin round so the driver can use the controls for both the front loader and the backhoe.

Auger The first type of auger was invented over 2000 years ago. Screws or spirals were used to lift water out of the ground, usually for farmers to use on their fields.

Bucket-wheel excavator These machines can be as long as a football pitch and as tall as a block of flats.

24